The Simple Reader's Guide to Understanding the Affordable Care Act (ACA) Health Care Reform

Denecia A. Jones

First Edition

abbott press®

A DIVISION OF WRITER'S DIGEST

Abbott Press books may be ordered through booksellers or by contacting:

Abbott Press
1663 Liberty Drive
Bloomington, IN 47403
www.abbottpress.com
Phone: 1-866-697-5310

ISBN: 978-1-4582-1082-1 (sc)
ISBN: 978-1-4582-1083-8 (hc)
ISBN: 978-1-4582-1084-5 (e)

Library of Congress Control Number: 2013914847

Printed in the United States of America.

Abbott Press rev. date: 8/29/2013

About the Author

Denecia A. Jones
CEO and Founder
D. A. Jones Insurance Services, Inc.

Denecia A. Jones is known by peers and clients alike for her integrity, responsiveness, and comprehensive insurance expertise. Mrs. Jones consistently focuses on developing long-term client relationships while remaining current with developments in the rapidly evolving insurance industry.

Health insurance reform is currently at a critical crossroads, and Mrs. Jones is committed to ensuring that her clients receive the best information possible in order to make educated decisions. For example, an increase in the Medicare wage tax to 3.8% was introduced in the year 2013, among other changes. In 2014 taxes imposed on nearly all private health insurance plans and in 2015 employers tax penalties of $2000 if they fail to offer insurance for each full-time employee.

Denecia A. Jones is well prepared to help her clients face these challenges. Born and raised in Los Angeles, she earned her Bachelor of Science degree in business administration from University of Phoenix and her master's degree in business management from Pepperdine University. She worked as a financial advisor with AIG, specializing in retirement, estate, and income replacement insurance and financial services. After her position at AIG, Mrs. Jones worked as a client financial analyst for Citibank. She founded D. A. Jones Insurance Services in September 2004, where she assists business owners with employer and employee insurance benefits, such as group and individual health insurance plans. Her firm also aids with implementing business protection plans as well as reducing business overhead costs.

Mrs. Jones is a certified estate planner, and her company is certified as a Woman and Minority Owned Business Enterprise. In addition, she is an active member of the National Association of Insurance and Financial Advisors (NAIFA) and the National Association of Health Underwriters (NAHU). Mrs. Jones actively gives back to the community, serving numerous non-profit organizations, including the AIDS Walk of Los Angeles; the Salvation Army of Southern California; the American Cancer Society; Rotary International; the National Multiple Sclerosis Society; Aids for AIDS, Nevada; Walk with Sally; and the Blind Children's Center of Los Angeles. In her spare time she enjoys yoga, hiking and traveling the world.

Her greatest investment of time and energy is directed toward ensuring that her clients' voices are heard during the most recent health care reform process. Mrs. Jones was one of the insurance advisors asked to meet with government representatives in Washington D.C., a meeting that had an enormous impact on the Affordable Care Act (ACA) Health Care Reform law. As an independent insurer and trusted advisor, she is proud to assist employers with issues related to the ACA prior to its full implementation in 2018.

Denecia A. Jones can be contacted by phone at 877-539-7701 or by email at denecia@dajonesinsurance.org. You can connect with her on Linked in at http://www.linkedin.com/in/djsworld. Mrs. Jones is available for speaking engagements.

Dedication:

Since the beginning of ACA in 2010, I have noticed that more and more people I meet don't understand this massive piece of legislation. I wrote this book to empower readers, so they understand the basics of this monumental health care law. I dedicate this book to all of the readers who have taken the first step to understand ACA Health Care Reform by reading my book. It will take some time to understand, but I promise you that if you read this book, you will be well on your way to understanding what and how the ACA will change the way the United States provides Health care.

I also dedicate this book to those who our dear to my heart my amazing husband Michael J. Todaro Jr., my family and my friends.

Thank you for your love and support.
Love,
Denecia A. Jones

Dear Readers,

ACA changes the way Americans receive health care by offering more competition and choice for families to make the best decision about the policies they think will best serve their needs. Americans who have pre-existing conditions and changed carriers or jobs will now be allowed to get access to care and can't be denied care based on those conditions. Seniors will receive billions of dollars in savings in prescription drug costs as a result of ACA, and many low income families who previously couldn't afford care will be able to get subsidies to help their families get the best care possible.

Americans can help with the ACA by first making sure they take the time to read and learn about all of the benefits the law provides for all Americans. The worst thing to do is to buy into the demagoguery used against the legislation by those looking to score political points. Americans should make sure they are informed and reach out to make sure they are taking advantage of all of the benefits ACA provides.

Sincerely,
Karen Bass
Congresswoman representing California's 37th District

Table of Contents

In this book you will learn about the history of health care reform and how the Affordable Care Act (ACA) will change health care in the United States. In order to understand the ACA Health Reform, I will first discuss the history of health care reform in the United States.

History of U.S Health Care Reform

Prior to the 1960s, seniors and the disabled did not receive health care to treat their health conditions because insurance plans were expensive and unaffordable to most. To fill the major void in the health care system, John F. Kennedy publicly discussed the concept of Medicare and Medicaid programs in 1962. With public support, Lyndon B. Johnson signed the amendment to the social security act, TITLE XVIII—Health Insurance For The Aged And Disabled, to the Social Security Act to add Medicare into our national health care system in 1965.

What is the difference between the Medicare and Medicaid? Medicare is our public health program that insures senior citizens and disabled people. Medicaid is our public health program that insures lower income individuals and their dependents as well as people with certain disabilities.

Health Maintenance Organization (HMO) Act of 1973

In 1973, President Richard Nixon signed the Health Maintenance Organization (HMO) Act of 1973. President Nixon helped fund the growth of the HMO system in the U.S. because he wanted to give Americans health insurance plan options. In President Nixon's statement on signing the HMO Act of 1973, he stated, "Health maintenance organizations provide health care to their members on a prepaid basis with emphasis on essential preventive services. The establishment of HMO's will allow people to select for themselves either a prepaid system for obtaining health services or the more traditional approach which has served the American people so well over the years." In the 1980s, HMOs plan options were a very popular plan design with employers. Today, the employer and individual plan market prefers PPO health insurance over HMO.[1]

Consolidated Omnibus Budget Reconciliation Act (COBRA)

Prior to the 1990s, employees who decided to leave their employer were not able to take their health insurance plans with them. For those individuals who had an illness or had dependents who were ill on the insurance plans, getting health insurance coverage elsewhere was not an option. In the individual and family health insurance market, if someone had an illness and did not have insurance to cover expenses, insurance carriers declined to offer them coverage. In other words, the healthy could get health insurance coverage after they were removed from their employer plan, and the ill were left in the cold. Because of this loophole in the health care system, the Consolidated Omnibus Budget Reconciliation Act (COBRA) was signed into law in 1996. COBRA requires employers to extend group health benefits to employees who may no longer work for the company but who still want to maintain and pay for their health insurance plans. I cannot imagine a world without COBRA and wonder how the ill workforce survived when their group plan coverage ended.

Children's Health Insurance Program (CHIP)

In 1997, voters approved the Children's Health Insurance Program (CHIP). This program helps cover children who lack private insurance. CHIP allows low- to moderate-income families the ability to provide health insurance to their children through this public program. The program was created because families were living uninsured, especially if they could not get their children insurance. The program allowed children to be covered free or at a low rate because the federal government subsidizes the cost to make it affordable. Today, The Children's Health Insurance Program (CHIP) provides health coverage to nearly 8 million children in families with incomes too high to qualify for Medicaid but who can't afford private coverage.[2]

Medicare Modernization Act (MMA)

In the early 2000s, The United States had a major dilemma with senior citizens. The costs of prescription drugs were very expensive for most people who did not have insurance. As a result, many seniors would travel across the U.S. border to Mexico and Canada to purchase more affordable drugs. I remember traveling to Costa Rica and meeting a citizen of Canada on my trip, and we started to discuss health care. He mentioned that seniors from the U.S. would go to use their health care system for the affordable drugs it offered to anyone so much that Canadians had to pay additional co-pays for drugs because there was a shortage for Canadians. I was very surprised. I never would have thought that in the golden years, the most established part of their lives for some, senior citizens would have to travel to another country to get prescription drugs because they simply could not pay the expensive rates for them in the United States. Once the United States was notified by Canada about the issue, Congress created a bill to resolve it.

The Medicare Modernization Act of 2003 (MMA) was created and approved by Congress. George W. Bush signed it into law that same year. The Medicare Modernization Act is also known as the Medicare Part D law; this program expanded prescription drug benefits to senior citizens. If a senior had the Medicare supplemental health insurance plan from an insurance carrier, that senior would also need to purchase a Medicare Part D health insurance plan and pay for drugs through that Part D plan. Senior citizens who purchased a Medicare supplemental plan who did not purchase a Part D at the time of the original enrollment would be subject to a penalty of 1%. "The late enrollment penalty is calculated by multiplying 1% of the "national base beneficiary premium" ($31.17 in 2013) times the number of full, uncovered months you were eligible but didn't join a Medicare Prescription Drug Plan and went without other creditable prescription drug coverage. The final amount is rounded to the nearest $.10 and added to your monthly premium."[3] Senior citizens who do not enroll in time and do so at a later date are unaware of this penalty until they enroll. Once enrolled, those seniors are notified by the Medicare Part D plan because their penalty is incorporated into their monthly premiums.

Affordable Care Act

If you are unaware of the true dilemma of our current health care system, here is the information you need to increase your knowledge. Health monthly premiums and health care expenses with insurance have skyrocketed in the past 10 years. When I say skyrocketed, I don't mean like a paper airplane flight only a few degree above the ground. When I say skyrocketed, I mean the cost of health care has gone straight up like watching a space shuttle flight flying straight into outer space. Our health care system cost is increasing so much that there is no end in sight. For example, "The Kaiser Family Foundation reported that from 1999 to 2009, health insurance premiums for families rose 131%." I am sure you are wondering if the ACA reform is helping with slowing down that increase. Based on reports, the answer is yes. Monthly premiums have increased due to additional benefits required by law, such as dependent coverage until 26 years old and maternity coverage on all policies. The cost has also increased because of the insurance taxes incorporated in the new insurance rates that are used to pay for establishing the federal and state health insurance exchanges. ACA rates have shown a track record of health care cost increases, but those increases are less than previous years. It may be because ACA took effect in the middle of one of our worst recessions, and it may be because the ACA requires insurance carriers to pay policy holders money back if they did not spend premiums on their claims, a process called medical rebates. Another reason the rates may be steadily increasing instead of the previous drastic increases is government monitoring on how much insurance carriers can increase policy holders health insurance premiums. In the end, The Kaiser Family Foundation has shown that whatever is being done, it is slowing down the cost of health care.

The one thing that we have to remember when we compare rates of increases is that no one can put a number of the amount of money it costs to maintain someone's life. Life is priceless. It is nearly impossible to explain the difference of inflation on a car versus inflation on adequate health care to maintain someone's lifestyle or life. These two things are not an apple-to-apple comparison. When you try to compare these two subjects, it is more like an apple to an elephant. The elephant will always be more expensive and breathtaking.

On March 23, 2010, President Barack Obama signed the Patient Protection and Affordable Care Act (PPACA), or ACA into law. The law includes numerous health-related provisions to take effect over an eight -year period, including prohibiting denial of coverage and claims based on pre-existing conditions, insurance taxes and penalties for insurance carriers, businesses, and individuals. ACA also expands Medicaid eligibility, subsidizes insurance premiums, provides incentives for businesses to provide health care benefits, and establishes health insurance exchanges and support for medical research. Senior citizens will see a discount of up to 53.5% for brand-name prescription drugs once they meet their drug plan deductible, also known as the prescription donut hole. [4]

Health Care System Past and Future

In the beginning of the Health Care System in the United States, the main objectives were to have a system that allowed physicians to assist their patients and insurance carriers to help both their community of patients and their doctors. One of the ways that insurance carriers did this was to create the prepaid health insurance plan where patients pay a monthly premium for their health insurance to pay for future health insurance expenses from a doctor or hospital. The insurance carriers would market doctors to new patients and remind patients of any out- of–pocket payment that was due to the physician(s). The setup was very simple when health insurance plans were first established over 200 years ago in the U.S.

As physicians' cost increased physicians increased their rates for services to pay for expenses. Soon after this change, patient ability to pay doctors became unmanageable. It was at this point that the insurance carriers got into the cost management side of the business. This portion of their business is when an insurance carrier reviews a physician's rate and study's the average rate in that physician's geographical area. Then the insurance carrier determines the in-network doctor's rate for that particular service, even if the doctor wants more money for that particular service.

Soon after this change of claim processing, physicians not only had difficulty collecting money for past services from patients, but also faced difficulty in collecting from insurance carriers on past services provided. During this time, physicians had the opportunity to work with pharmaceutical companies on making additional streams of income by prescribing prescription drugs to patients. Physicians not only got money back for drugs prescribed, but there also were nice trips and kickbacks given to them by pharmaceutical companies. For a short time, these helped physicians with supplementing their income until now.

You see, part of the reason health care costs are so high is many Americans use prescription drugs. As a result, the cost of prescription medications spending in the U.S. was $259.1 billion in 2010 and is projected to double over the next decade.[5] The current rate of growth has slowed from the highs of the 1990s and early 2000s to a more modest rate, but it is expected to increase sharply in 2014 after the individual and family insurance coverage mandate in each state becomes effective. In 2010, 90% of seniors and 57% of non-elderly adults had a prescription drug expense.[6] Additionally, as the number of medicines being prescribed increased: from 1999 to 2011, the number of prescriptions rose 43% (from 2.8 billion to 4 billion), outpacing U.S. population growth by 9%.[7] Although still only a modest part of total health care spending in the U.S (10%), with so many people relying on prescriptions, the cost implications loom large for the American public and health insurers.

Prescription drugs are a huge cost to health insurance carriers. One of the things we will see to reduce the cost is tier prescription drug models that are manage by pharmaceutical providers like CVS and Express Script. These providers create a tier system that allows patients to get brand-name prescriptions only by moving up through several tiers of preferred generic drugs before they are all allowed to purchase expensive brand-name prescription drugs.

I had the chance to check out the system myself in the spring of 2013. I was on a brand-name drug for acid reflux for a year through the insurance of my husband's old employer when he enrolled to the same insurance carrier in a PPO plan similar to what we had before. However, this plan had a different pharmaceutical administrative company. My access to the brand-name drug that I had been using was now denied. When I asked why the pharmaceutical administrative company denied it, they said it was because I had not gone through the lowest tier yet. When I asked for clarification, they told me that I needed to try a prescription drug- generic prescription tier 1 and if the drug wasn't effective, I would need to go through the appeal process. Once the appeal process was complete on my end and approved on theirs, they would allow me to go to the next tier. This tier contained strengthened versions of the first tier drugs. When I asked how many tiers it would take for me to appeal to get brand-name drugs, I was told three.

I was very unhappy with this approach and the results. I personally don't like taking prescription drugs for any reason unless I need them to function. I only wanted to function on my healthy diet without feeling like my digestive system was in pain all the time. So for the next few months, I was busy going through the appeal process. My doctor had to submit the appeal paperwork to the pharmacy and the pharmaceutical administrative company. Then we would just wait to make sure they received proper paperwork and make a decision on my request for an appeal. The Pharmaceutical administrator approved my third request for appeal in three months. I was glad they approved my request but I was very disappointed with the process.

From a company perspective, I understand that they were trying to cut health care costs for everyone by using this system that has been utilized by the military for many years. On a consumer side, my husband and I pay for our own health care through his employer.

If the company wants happy employees, then their best bet is to not give the wife of an employee the run around when she needs her existing prescription drugs. The company has since changed the pharmaceutical administrator due to employee complaints. It was nice to know that I was not the only one who had an issue with the new drug tier system. It is also nice to know that my husband's employer acknowledged and changed company policy to make sure staff and their families were happy with the results. In this case, change was a good thing.

Today, a once simplified health insurance system is so complicated that it took the U.S. government months to create a 1000-page document explaining the new PPACA health care reform law. Consumers who once trusted the insurance carriers and saw them as the hero when consumers needed to use their insurance are now weary after past reports show that insurance carriers drop ill patients from insurance policies. Granted, there were some individuals who falsified information on their applications, such as not disclosing illnesses that were required by law, and the carrier would drop coverage and retroactively collect the amounts covered by the insurance. However, some of the people who the insurance carriers dropped did not falsify their applications.

Physicians and Hospitals

When the American health care system was created many decades ago, a physician's main purpose was to heal the ill with traditional Western medicine. The American Medical Association (AMA) was created by physicians to find ways to best care for people in each community. Prior to the formation of AMA, physicians had an issue with providing care to clients who had no money to pay for their care. The dilemma for physicians was that they weren't able to pay their business expenses to continue caring for their clients. As a solution to the issue, the first health insurance plan was established in Houston, Texas. Blue Cross was a prepaid health insurance program similar to what most Americans use on a daily basis today. The goal of the plan was to help physicians receive payment for services prior to patient visits. It helped patients with a pay-as-you-go plan that was strictly used for medical expenses.

This program was such a success that it spread across the nation like a wild fire. With new regional locations being added to the program and new insurance carriers repeating the same structure or creating alterations to the structure, insurance carriers became the heroes of the communities in which they worked. They helped connect physicians and hospitals for the purpose of helping the community by caring for the ill. This concept created a way to see the patients before they were chronically ill. Today, physicians' current insurance payments that they once applauded have shrunk, and as a result, physicians and hospitals get less reimbursement for their provided services. Furthermore, most physicians and hospitals must have a staff or collection agency to collect the payment promised by the insurance carriers for the services. As a result, these solution increase that physician expenses and pressure to see more patients or find alternative routes to increase their revenue.

Concierge Medicine

There are physicians who have had enough of the nonsense and want to focus on patient care and take control of their finances. These physicians have joined the Concierge Medicine Movement. Concierge Medicine allows physicians to offer their patients the ability to receive exclusive member benefits for a membership fee. The way that it works is that the physician must be a member of a Concierge Medicine Group and the patient would become a "wellness club" member in the physician's network.

Patient benefits as a member of a Concierge Medicine Group include the following:

- Visit doctors more often if needed

- Same-day doctor visits

- More time with doctor during visits

In the end, the program allows patients who can afford an annual fee of $1800-$2500 to get faster service, receive more personal care, and see their doctor more often than a non-member.

Physician benefits as a member of Concierge Medicine Group include the following:

- Additional income stream outside of the insurance carriers

- More time to connect with patients to focus on wellness and quality of care

- Reduced dependence on payments from insurance reimbursements for services rendered

Concierge Medicine has been around for the last few years but has had positive results so far. According to the AMA, Concierge Medicine has resulted in a 79% reduction in hospital admission and has improved management of chronic conditions. I was unable to find any other associations or organizations that can support or oppose AMA's statement.[8]

I have a dear friend who signed up for Concierge Medicine because his physician told him that, "he would only take patients who were members." I asked him what his thoughts about the program were, and he said it is great. He mentioned that he is able to see the physician who he has been with for over 20 years, and the type of care his doctor gives him is much better than with his insurance plan only. In his words, it is "well worth the money."

The controversy is that some believe this type of care is an unfair way of allowing physicians to choose to care for rich patients and eliminate the poor. The last time I checked, I live in The United States of America, a place where citizens have the right to have a freedom of speech and choice. Unless there is a law that outlaws having a choice in choosing cliental that a doctor selects, then it is not illegal, and physicians should be free to do whatever they believe is a good fit for their own practices. Do not get me wrong, it may not be a fair practice that physicians choose to stop or not care for the poor or less fortunate, but it's their choice as business owners and an integral part of keeping people in communities healthy. The question, I ask those who do not support that right, is if you were a physician and your income was being reduced but your bills continued to increase, what would you do to increase your income and provide better care for your patients?

Another option for those who are concerned about the ACA reform and the major changes with the payment structure of reimbursements is membership in a physicians' association. These associations are formed to provide a support networks for small-to mid-sized physicians for various items. One of the physicians associations that I interviewed was Private Practice Doctors (PPD) located in Beverly Hills, California. PPD is a management association created by a group of physicians who have a vision to collaborate with other physicians to lower business expenses by merging their practices into one organization. PPD leverages the buying power of its physician members. The goal is to spend less time and money managing their administrative needs and increase time with their patients. PPD offers their physician members the following:

- Group Purchasing

- Electronic Medical Records

- Billing Services

- Insurance for Office Staff

- Banking Services

Physicians who want to be a part of these benefits are joining associations like PPD on a regular basis as a way to adapt to changes in the health care system.

Physicians' View Point

I had a chance to interview Private Practice Doctors (PPD) to discuss the changes that they have experienced with ACA reform. As far as membership demographics, most of the member physicians have had their practices for 10-30 years. Most of the member doctors have their practices in Beverly Hills or the surrounding areas, which are high income cliental from Los Angeles County. It was for these reasons that physicians accepted mostly PPO insurance plans. The PPD member demographic mostly consists of physicians who work at UCLA, Cedar Sinai, and Saint John's hospital. After ACA was signed into law in 2010, member physicians noticed private and Medicare insurance reimbursements were being reduced while overhead costs, such as banking services and credit card processing fees, increased. As a way to adapt, physicians began to share office space. When that did not work, they eliminated their in-house medical labs and began to outsource for a fee. When that didn't work, the same group of physicians created PPD in 2011. Dr. Reed Wilson, a cardiologist, is the CEO of PPD. He stated, "The challenges are not just in overhead changes and reimbursements. It's also in the way that physicians work with clients." ACA has created more regulations in patient care, which creates a challenge to maintain patients. Alexandra, a member of the PPD team mentioned that, "Even if a physician is a specialist, as opposed to a generalist, they get paid the same with the new reimbursement fees. That is so hard to believe. Why would a physician remain or strive to become a provider of specialty care?

When I mentioned Accountability Care Organizations (ACO) and solicited PPD's thoughts about the new health care model created by the U.S. Government's Department of Health and Human Services, she said, "Our physicians don't want to be a part of an ACO, bought out by a big hospitals or a member of Concierge Medicine group, they want to remain in private practice. They want to provide the care their patients deserve." Today, PPD has over 200 members who joined in hopes of being proactive to adapt and remain in business as private practices.

Medical Trends

In the past 20 years, I have met some doctors who have gotten into the medical profession just to get rich. They spent their time seeing patients and prescribing expensive procedures that they knew were not normally approved as a covered benefit by the patient insurance carriers. They also would make money by prescribing prescription drugs to patients to get extra bonuses and perks from pharmaceutical companies prior to government regulations eliminating these practices. In 2013, a study from Mayo Clinic researchers reveals that 7 out of 10 Americans take at least one prescription drug.[9] Some of these illnesses can be treated simply by a change of diet and engaging in exercise. As a result, most Americans are accustomed to taking medications to feel better even if drugs are not needed to recover from an illness.

The cost of drugs in the health care system is one of the reasons the U.S health care system is going broke. How? Too much money is paid out and not enough revenue is paid into insurance systems to pay claims and administrative costs. It may be because for the past two decades Americans were not encouraged to live healthier lives but somehow with the help of drugs are living much longer than previous generations. As a result of the broken health care system insurance carriers are pointing their fingers at the physicians who once focused on the care of the patients in the community but who no longer could keep their doors open with the amount they were getting reimbursed. The insurance carriers wonder why some doctors jump at the chance to make money if they prescribe prescription drugs. In a way to change the health care system the US Government plans is to restructure America's health care system in an attempt to improve physician and patient care with the ACA.

With all these changes in the health care system, I wanted to know what changes patients will notice in the next year. To find the answer to those questions and others that relate to doctors, I sought out Dr. Stanley Hubbard from UCLA Medical Group in Santa Monica. I asked three questions. 1) How is health care reform affecting his practice, and 2) What are major changes you predict will happen with regards to the current physician and hospital climate and why? 3) What he thought would be the expectations of a new physician compared to someone who has been in the industry for 10 or 20 years?

In response to the first question, Dr. Hubbard said the ACA health care reform has not affected his practice. What has affected his practice is UCLA and Blue Shield of California were unable to agree on renewing their contract and as a result, we have lost many of our patients. In his response to the second question, he stated, "Hospitals work like hotels." The medical groups have found it more advantageous to use hospitals. For example, hospitals have a discharge time. It is more beneficial to have the patients who are on the route to be discharged to be discharged in the morning. Doctors who work in a hospital, also known as "Hospitalist" are more effective at getting those patients out of the hospital than those who work in an office outside of a hospital. The doctors who work in an outside office have to make time to go to the hospital and sometimes do not arrive until after 11am. By that time, the patient's insurance is charged an additional day even when the patient is discharged the same day. It is for this reason that the newest health care trend is Hospitalist as the most efficient method of care. I further asked what UCLA is doing to adapt to health care reform in order to better serve its patients? Dr. Hubbard answered that computers are being used more, which makes things more efficient and gives doctors time to provide better care for patients.

I then asked him, "What do you think would be the expectations of a new physician compared to someone who has been in the industry for 10 or 20 years? In his reply, he said that, in the old days, doctors were looked at as artists of medicine. "Many doctors in the old days, it was deductive reasoning. Today a physician's decision is based on evidence that can only be received from taking tests."

Some patients wonder why their physicians have to give them many tests before recommending a treatment. The main reason is malpractice. A physician has a patient take more tests to reduce their malpractice liability and ensures the patient's health condition is based on factual and verifiable results.

Bi-Socialized Medicine

Some media outlets have said that this is the end of the private insurance system era as we know it, and I agree with that point of view. It is the end because the past system was no longer working for most of the people it was designed to serve both patients and physicians. The ACA system that we have entered is a new era of socialized medicine called "bi-socialized medicine." Socialized medicine is defined as medical and hospital services for the members of a class or population administered by an organized group (as a state agency) and paid for from funds obtained usually by assessments, philanthropy, or taxation. "Bi-socialized medicine" is when a government entity and insurance carriers collaboratively work toward socializing a health care market with private income and public taxation. This type of medicine differs from other countries for example England health was a health care system is socialized. Socialized is where the government is the primarily creator and charges the taxpayers for their health insurance while the insurance companies supplement whatever is not covered. Bi-socialized medicine is when the government makes laws that affect the insurance market while benefiting from revenue into the existing governmentally established plans. In this case the existing governmental plan is Medicare.

Bi-Socialized is a unique system that has not been seen anywhere in the world. It may be considered by some as an innovative and collaborative effort to improve the existing private and public health care systems.

Agents and Navigators

In 2014, there are several resources consumers can go to for answers on how to purchase health insurance: agents and navigators. A common question that I get from consumers and other insurance agents asks what the difference is between the two.

Agents are licensed professionals who are registered with their state's department of insurance. These people are fingerprinted and required to complete insurance continuing education, including ethics classes. Each state's department of insurance keeps files on these people, including any complaints. Agents are compensated for their expertise and assistance to clients by commissions. Most agents are individuals who build relationships with their clients and can provide advice on the policy that best meets each person's needs.

Navigators are a new concept that was created under ACA. Navigators are individuals who are not required to hold insurance licenses or any licenses at all. They are not subject to background checks or any formal registration. They will be required to go through some training, but they cannot offer advice or guidance on which plan to select. Navigators are projected to be compensated by a salary plus commission for each policy placed. Their salaries are funded by state and federal tax dollars. California estimates that it will need 21,000 navigators to connect with the insured market starting in 2014. Navigators can be anywhere from a grocery store to a call center or the shopping mall to help get people signed up more easily.

Keep in mind that either person you work with will have access to your personal information as you will provide it, and as of today, neither will be able to sell a government policy. Most importantly, be sure to ask questions and work with someone you feel you can trust and has your best interest in mind.

What Will Happen to Our Health Care System?

The health care system we once knew will be gone with a blink of the eye. Physicians who don't want to deal with the constant hassle of caring for patients from the insurance carriers who are consistently focused on lowering costs, not the care of the patient, are retiring. Those who become doctors will treat more patients with Western Medicine while getting paid less than before. Other physicians will choose to take their patients to concierge services and say goodbye to partnering with insurance carriers.

Insurance carriers are far less interested in incorporating Eastern medicine methods, such as chiropractic medicine, acupuncture, and massage, to resolve patient illnesses than exercise or eating right. Eating right is also a huge part of herbal medicines, which is a large market and has a history of results, but insurance carriers are not so sure that they want to insure these methods. Why? It is simply because they don't understand them. Until they are able to do so, insurance carriers are missing opportunities to improve the health of people in the communities that once honored them in helping physicians with the dilemma of patient payment and care.

In 2015, I predict that the number of hospitals will decrease because of government regulations, cost of overhead and caring for patients, and payments received that do not cover all their expenses. More doctors will provide out-patient, in-home care to patients. Doctors will be able to run their offices on the road with electronic medical systems, improved IT, and enhanced health insurance patient protection and security measured access. What does this mean? It means that hospitals will be used strictly for overnight stays and surgeries because the doctor-patient ratio will be changing. Doctors who have more patients will also have regulations that will supposedly reduce insurance costs as well but may increase wait times for patients who need surgeries. For patients who are okay with waiting for major care, great. For those who are not, insurance carriers may offer a supplement or enhanced plan that reduces wait times if the patients are willing to pay higher monthly premiums and reimbursements.

Some people are going aboard for their surgical treatment. An up-and-coming alternative that is here is American-trained doctor treatment cruises. You pay a certain price of the procedure in the U.S., such as for heart surgery, hip replacement, or cancer removal. If one goes on a cruise ship vacation near Thailand, you can have your procedure and recovery time on a luxury ship strictly for medical treatment for a discounted rate. Some doctors from other countries are doing quite well with this method. The catch for patients is that there are no regulations of proper care based on U.S. standards because once out of the country, one is in international waters. This means there are alternatives to reducing cost of surgical care, but they come with risk.

ACA Affordable Health Care?

Even though the U.S. government promises affordable insurance, the truth is that they are right that the insurance is affordable for low income and poor but for the rest of the population affordable depends on who you talk to that day. Are the premiums affordable for them? For you? For a select group of people with certain incomes

The main goal of health care reform with ACA is to cut health care costs by stabilizing rates. One of the ways to stabilize rates is to change the way physicians work with patients. In the past, physicians would prescribe prescription drugs to resolve a health issue, propose a surgery, and or refer the patient to a specialist. Physicians refer patients to other physicians who are a specialist in a certain area and have expertise in that field. The new way that physicians will help patients is to let the patients find their own specialist, get healthier so that they are not dependent on prescription drugs, and order surgery only if a patient absolutely needs it. The time that a patient is held in a hospital or outpatient facility will be reduced to also cut health care cost.

It has been long-term knowledge that most people heal better when they are in their homes as opposed to a germ-filled hospital or facility. It also costs a lot less for physicians and insurance carriers, as well as patients, if they are treated in their homes instead of a hospital or facility. I believe the days when doctors did house calls overseas may be here in the U.S. It is a way to cut health care costs and add patient convenience.

Individual and Family Plans after ACA

For the past 100 years, insurance was primarily sold by a human, an insurance agent. An insurance agent would relay the insurance carrier benefits, rates, and exclusions to consumers prior to finding the best plan that fit that client needs. With the changes in technology, consumers can go on the Internet and purchase their own policies. Many people forget to read the exclusions, or they do not understand when a policy's benefit change occurs what the change is and how it will affect them.

On a daily basis, I have had clients come to me who had self-purchased insurance plans online and did not realize a benefit they needed was no longer covered with that plan. Most of the time, I am assisting clients with understanding the ins and outs of their plan benefits and making sure that it's a good fit for their objectives. In 2014, the U.S. government requires insurance carriers to offer a standard set of insurance benefits, called" Essential Health Benefits," when a consumer purchases a health insurance plan. An example of Essential Health Benefits is an applicant receiving "Guaranteed Issuances" for individuals and families. What "Guaranteed Issuances" means is that applicants are insurable no matter what illnesses that they may have at that time. Even if the applicant has a life-threatening illness, that applicant will not be declined insurance coverage by that health insurance carrier. In translation, for the government this means that insurance coverage must be offered to all Americans.

Grandfathered and
Non-Grandfathered Plans

Some individuals and groups have asked me what the difference is between "Grandfathered" and "Non-Grandfathered plans." A Grandfathered plan is a plan that was purchased by a business as their group plan or by an individual or family prior to ACA being signed into law. ACA was signed into law on March 10, 2010. These plans are Grandfathered in because the policy holder can keep the plan through the implementation of new plan designs that include "Essential Health Benefits" in January 2014. In other words, these policy holders can elect to keep their Grandfathered plans that do not have Essential Health Benefits in them after January 2014.

So you are probably wondering what happens to the policy of those who purchased their plans after ACA was signed into law? These plans are considered "non-Grandfathered plans." In January 2014, these plans will no longer be available to policy holders because ACA requires minimum coverage requirements given to policy owners, and these non-Grandfathered plans currently do not have these benefits in them. What this means for policy owners is that prior to January 2014, your insurance carrier will send you a letter offering you new plan options, and you and your agent will review the benefits and rates to find a plan that best fits your needs. Some insurance carriers already have plans and rates with the new plans ready for purchase, and others will have them ready for purchase as soon as Fall 2013. In Summer of 2013 insurance carriers gave a new renewal option for Grand-fathered policy holders. A group health insurance policy holder can extend their plan another year past January 2014. For example, a group client whose group renewal is in January 1, 2014 that client's insurance carrier is offering to extend their renewal to January 1, 2015. After January 2015 that group will need to switch to a new plan option that includes ACA Essential Health Benefits. In the end, the last quarter of 2013 will be a very busy time for the government, insurance carriers, business owners, and individuals because of the ACA mandates.

Guaranteed Issuance

Some people I have talked to believe the ACA will allow them to purchased affordable insurance that they could not buy before for a cheap rate, as they were declined coverage because of a preexisting health condition. Even though the intentions behind the ACA legislation may have been to provide affordable rates and guaranteed insurance coverage for individuals and families to purchase health insurance, insurance carriers will continue to be very careful about protecting their existing policyholders from rate increases. These increases will come when too many ill policyholders are offered coverage under ACA's guaranteed insurance provision. The insurance carriers' translation of the ACA's guaranteed issuance provisions is not to decline an applicant. However, insurance carriers have the right to charge the applicant with a critical illness an additional surcharge on the original quoted rate. An example of this would be one of my clients seeking a policy for her son who had cancer five years ago. The first carrier we applied to approved us. When I asked, the rate the carrier mentioned it was at 100% more than the original premium. Therefore, for a $300 policy, they would have charged us $600 a month. I kindly passed on the "amazing" offer, and I went to another carrier who offered us the original rate without an increase.

Guaranteed Issuance health insurance is a new option for those individuals who may not have been insurable due to a health issue. Buyer must be aware that insurance coverage options in 2014 for those who are ill may not be at an affordable rate.

Balance of Cost and Patient Care

The way that we see our health care system is changing. Why? Because the cost of health care is getting more expensive every day, so much that insurance carriers and the government are at a point where the cost charged to patients is not covering the cost of medical expenses or operational maintenance costs. Even though plan benefits not covered today may be covered tomorrow, we will see insurance carriers reliant on physicians for changing the way Americans receive health care. Some examples of these changes are electronic medical record systems, restrictions on appealing a pharmacy declination of brand-name prescription drugs for a member, and encouraging physicians to not refer a patient to a specialist.

Electronic medical record systems will reduce paper waste and allow various departments to impact patient care in a doctor's office or hospital. The only concern for some is will all electronic medical systems communicate with other hospitals or doctors' office besides the originator. If so, then how does this system make it safe for patient information by having to transport data electronically? These are the types of questions that U.S. government, physicians, health insurance carriers, and patients have not yet been able to answer.

Senior Citizens

The health reform will be an adjustment for senior citizens in the U.S. The population 65 years and over has increased from 35 million in 2000 to 40 million in 2010 (a 15% increase) and is projected to increase to 55 million in 2020. This is a 36% increase for that decade.[10]

Since 1900, the percentage of Americans 65+ has more than tripled (from 4.1% in 1900 to 13.1% in 2010), and the number has increased almost 13 times from 3.1 million to 40.4 million. [11]

With the help of advancement in medicine, people are living longer and healthier than previous generations. In 2013, seniors represented 12.9% of the *U.S. population,* about one in every eight Americans. [12] The senior market is an important part of our economy, and if they aren't happy with associations like AARP or the government, senior advocacy group are not afraid to let an organization know. In the health insurance coverage with seniors as of 2010, "almost all (93.1%) non-institutionalized persons 65+ were covered by Medicare. Medicare covers mostly acute care services and requires beneficiaries to pay part of the cost, leaving about half of health spending to be covered by other sources. About 58% of seniors had some type of private health insurance. Over 8% had military-based health insurance and 9% of the non-institutionalized elderly were covered by Medicaid. Less than 1% did not have coverage of some kind." [13]

In the past, the high cost of prescription drugs drove seniors to go elsewhere to get the drugs they needed at a very low cost. As I mentioned before in the history of health care reform, in 2003, George W. Bush signed a health care reform bill called Medicare Modernization Act of 2003 (MMA). The MMA was created and approved by Congress and signed into law that same year by President George W. Bush. The MMA is also known as Medicare Part D law: This law required senior citizens to purchase their prescription drugs in the U.S. If seniors did not, they would be required to pay a penalty of 1% of their income each year. The government created Part D because it was planned to reduce prescription drug costs. Does this idea sound familiar?

Health care reform supporters mention a very similar message. After several years of senior clients who helped enroll and maintain their Medicare supplement and part of prescription drug plans, the general public noticed that Medicare Part D was charging seniors the retail price for their drugs, which is extremely expensive. Medicare Part D did supplement the cost once the client met the plan deductible, which in this case was called a plan donut hole. However, prior to meeting this requirement, seniors would sometimes pay $500-$1000 per prescription. In translation, the seniors signed up for the Medicare supplement program and the prescription drug program. They would save on the monthly premium compared to being on a private health insurance plan. The new major cost would be paying the sometimes-high cost for their prescription drugs. If a senior did not have money saved or available for the required drugs then they did have access to cheaper generic alternatives. If there wasn't a generic drug option, then they had no other choice but to pay the retail price for their prescription drug. After years of complaints from seniors about the expense of drugs on Part D, the U.S. government added a revision in ACA.

Senior citizens can now get rebates on the amount spent on their drugs. Pharmaceutical companies also agreed to provide some brand-name drugs at discounted rates. This provision of Part D is making many senior citizens happy. Some say that provisions of the bill are the reason why seniors supported the ACA. The majority population supporting the bill was essential to gaining support from individual members of Congress, who dealt with early complaints from seniors during the health care reform debate. It is good to know that some government officials who are serving our country are listening.

Throughout the years, every country has come to really appreciate the voice of seniors. Our country has grown so much, and thankfully, each generation has learned from the previous ones. Senior citizens have lived through so much and have adapted to the changes. Seniors who stand up for what is right for our citizens and senior citizens alike inspire me every day. They provide me with courage to do what I do every day; to do what is right for my clients and protect them from harm. I am so happy that I have the opportunity to learn from their courage and show future generations the importance to do the same.

Few things have changed in laws prior to health reform. With the changes of reform, Senior Citizens on an employer plan, in some states, will not have an option to stay on their employer's group plan. Those senior citizens only have the option to enroll in Medicare. For example, Californian employers are allowed to move a senior from a private group plan to Medicare once that senior is eligible for Medicare benefits. This regulation assists employers with hundreds, if not thousands of dollars in reductions from their employer contributions toward the entire group health insurance plan. Senior citizens who make the switch also save money. One of the employers that I assist with group health insurance is saving nearly $15,000 a year now that I enrolled his Medicare eligible employee onto Medicare. Seniors also pay less for co-pays and out of pocket for medical expenses on Medicare especially if they are taking generic drugs.

Accountable Care Organizations (ACO)

The U.S. Government plans to reduce the overall cost of Medicare because of new detection systems in place that will quickly find duplicate and false claims. For example, the center of Medicare services has created Accountable Care Organizations (ACO). This Medicare model will work with physicians, hospitals, and health care practitioners to find a way to get Medicare patients coordinated care between their health care representatives at the low cost while avoiding unnecessary treatment, service duplication, and medical errors. A goal of an ACO is to give seniors the best care without unnecessarily overspending on health care that seniors do not need.

Some are not a fan of the new ACO model. In an article written in the Wall Street Journal, the writer mentioned that ACO is an interesting health care model. "Think about that one: The ACO model works because ACO patients are treated by ACO physicians. Yet this rule is written to ensure that seniors can take 'advantage of the full range of benefits to which they are entitled under Medicare, including the right to choose between health care providers and care settings.' So ACOs are going to transform health care, but individual patients don't need to be part of the transformation if they don't feel like it." [14]ACOs are known to cut cost, but at what cost will the patient care pay to save the hospital, government, and insurance carrier money? The answer to this question will soon come once there are more ACO results available after 2014.

Businesses and ACA

According to the U.S. Census data, 98% of businesses in the U.S. are small businesses with fewer than 100 employees. With the ACA, employers with more than 50 Full time Equivalent employees (FTE) will be required to pay a penalty for employees who they do not purchase health insurance for in 2015. A new phrase that I learned recently from an associate of mine is "Play or pay." When an employer decides to pay for health insurance for their staff it is called "play" because the employer will play by the ACA regulations. Employers who do not want to "Play" by the ACA regulations will "Pay" the health insurance penalty for each Full Time Equivalent (FTE). So you are probably wondering what is full time equivalent? It is a calculation that will determine if an employer is required to buy insurance or pay a tax penalty for not offering the insurance. The way FTE works is that the employer, who is required to calculate the full-time employees and then add the number of hours, must also add the number of part-time employees to this number. For example, if a company has two part-time employees working 20 hours a week, with the FTE calculation, those two part-time employees' hours are equivalent to one full-time employee. The FTE closes the loophole that businesses thought they had to maintain the workforce without having to offer health insurance benefits for the staff. The FTE also applies to companies that hire part-time seasonal employees. If an employee's hours surpasses 2,080 hour per year, that employee is an FTE.

Even though companies with less than 100 employees are defined as small businesses, the ACA defines companies that have more than 50 full-time employees or more than 50 Full-Time Equivalent (FTE) employees as large business also known as large group. In 2015, these businesses will be required to purchase health insurance for FTE employees or pay a tax penalty if they don't.

You are likely wondering why the full-time equivalent standard was created? In 2006, Massachusetts Governor Mitt Romney signed the Massachusetts Health Care Insurance Reform Law. The State of Massachusetts, who managed the regulations and implementation requirements for the law, made this requirement public, and the media began to interview companies about their thoughts about the new regulation. Some business owners and professionals decided to make public announcements that they would avoid the law by switching their full-time employees to part-time employees and just have more of them. Approximately two weeks later, Massachusetts state officials from the Department of Revenue adjusted the law and revised the full-time requirement to include full-time equivalents (FTEs).[15]

Since FTEs were a successful part of the Massachusetts health reform mandates the U.S. government has implemented FTE on a federal level by including it in ACA.

ACA Health Care Reform and Business Response

Many large businesses, such as Walmart, Papa John's pizza, and Regal Cinema Group, have made it public that they will continue to their businesses health care plans as usual. The only change that they will make to adapt with the ACA is cutting their workforce in half and cutting hours offered to staff.[16] They are not willing to invest in the new law because it will affect the way they do business. Then what happens to their employees who are not eligible for health insurance benefits through the ACA?

The employees who are not able to afford group insurance plans are likely to enroll in an individual health insurance plan or Medicaid. The Medicaid program is a federal program that is funded by taxpayers for those applicants for are make incomes less than the Federal Poverty Levels (FPL).The United States definition of poverty is defined each year by the Department of Health and Human Services (HHS).Health and Human Services manages federal programs such as Medicare, Medicaid, ACA and many more. Health and Human Services will expand Medicaid beginning January 2014. Medicaid will be available to adults under 138% of the federal poverty level who are American citizens. In 2013 the Federal Poverty Level was 1 person making $11,490, a 2 person family making $15,510 and a 3 person family making $19,530.

There is a risk that both small and large businesses will reduce employee hours to eliminate the requirement of offering health insurance to staff. I already have seen more and more job applicants wondering why they can't find full-time work. When I give them creative ideas about working two jobs or ways to start a business, they do not want to hear it.

Change is difficult for most people and that is understandable. In the end those who put the energy in understanding and adapting to change will be healthier and happier than others. Long story short, it is likely that companies will adapt to the regulations and have their W-2 employees work less. As a result, most employees will have to work two part-time jobs to equal the income of one, become 1099 workers or independent consultants.

The businesses that can afford and understand the value of their employees' increased loyalty, performance and dedication to the company in their work will pay to continue with the new ACA regulations in and after 2015. Many small and large businesses will pay for insurance to maintain their happy staff instead of paying the IRS tax penalties for not offering the large group health insurance benefits even if the penalty is less.

What many businesses owners don't understand is to look at things from an overall view. Paying to make sure staffs have adequate health insurance and being able to deduct those contributions opposed to paying a lesser amount with a tax penalty and eliminating that tax deduction is sometimes more costly then the savings that most companies had expected. I am not an accountant, but I advise companies to take that into consideration when they make their final decision. Now if a company simply cannot afford the increase in cost, then that is understandable, but if the employer is looking at things from a comparison standpoint, there is no comparison between the two.

Let's take a look a large group client's options with regard to health insurance options in 2014 and beyond.

Large groups will have three options to choose from with the ACA in 2015.

The first option for employers is to purchase the insurance in or outside of a health insurance exchange. A health insurance exchange will be a place where employers and employees can purchase their group health insurance plans online. A Private Health Exchange is owned and operated by a private or publically held organization. With this option, the employer will purchase a plan through a Private Exchange administrator who manages the rates, plan benefits, and billing for that employer. Usually, there is a minimum fee for clients to participate, and the Private Exchange is compensated by the insurance commissions that were purchased by that employer and or an employer administration fee.

The next option is to purchase health insurance through a Public Exchange. Public Exchanges are established, owned, and operated by a state or federal government agency. Public Exchanges are usually funded by tax monies. A few examples of the exchanges are in California, where the public exchange is Covered California; in Utah, where the public exchange is Avenue H; and in Massachusetts, where the public exchange is the Health Connector. Public Exchanges such as those mentioned are also a place where individual employees can get a federal subsidy, also known as a tax credit, if they are considered low income. Employees who decide to waive coverage through an employer plan may not qualify for a federal subsidy to purchase an individual health insurance plan. A federal subsidy will be given to individuals who do not have a group insurance plan option available and who have not waived coverage.

Another option is the employer purchase health insurance plans through a carrier directly opposed to going through an exchange.

The fourth option is to pay a tax penalty for each employee instead of offering health insurance. Some employers are focusing on this option because, in some cases, paying a tax penalty will cost them less than paying for the group health insurance contribution and additional Human Resource staff to manage the ACA's mandates. Keep in mind that there are insurance carriers who are offering insurance plans that will cost approximately the same as the cost of paying the tax penalty.

What are some employers doing about the ACA mandates? I interviewed Callan Carter, JD, an employee benefits attorney at Fisher & Phillips LLP, a professional law group. Callan Carter represents employers nationally in labor and employment matters. She also specializes in tax law. As a benefits attorney, she consults with her clients, employers, and plan sponsors on the sponsorship and administration of the benefits plans, both health and welfare and retirement incentives. With regard to the ACA, she assists her clients to keep up to date with her and clients' benefits plans in their compliance with any new requirements or changes. Mrs. Callan said she does not believe that ACA requirements outside of the "play or pay" provision have affected business operations. There are new and different employee notices, but those are just end up as more compliance items for benefits personnel to maintain.

With regard to the "play or pay" provision of ACA, in the process of dealing with her prospective and existing clients she stated, "I have seen quite a few reactions to ACA. For example, she has had two clients break up their control group by selling off ownership interests to make the resulting companies "small" and exempt from ACA."

When I asked Mrs. Carter on ways she has seen businesses change how they operate, she gave me several examples. "I have seen some business owners who are assuming the risk of an ERISA 510 claim. ERISA 510 makes it unlawful for any person to discharge, fine, suspend, expel, discipline, or discriminate against a participant or beneficiary for exercising any right to which he is entitled or may become entitled under an ERISA plan. It also makes it unlawful to discharge, fine, suspend, expel, or discriminate against any person because he has given information or has or is about to testify in any ERISA-related inquiry or proceeding." One anticipated example that would generate a complaint under ERISA is an employer firing an employee right before he or she becomes vested in a pension benefit so that he or she will not vest. Another example would be an employer reducing an existing employee's hours below 30 hours to keep him or her from continuing to be or becoming eligible (after January 2015) under the medical plan, that employee.

"As a concern to the ERISA 510 and ACA some employers are already responding by reducing existing employee hours to a maximum of 29 per week and hiring more part-time employees. Other businesses are placing a 29 hour per week maximum on new hires. Both of these strategies require more employees to do the existing work, so they are hiring and training more employees."

She went on to mention, "Of course, not all business lend themselves to a majority part-time population. Some businesses are already 'playing' or have to make very few changes to play so they are planning to make necessary changes to play. One of her clients who do not provide health insurance plans to staff rather than pay because it will actually be cheaper for the client will offer health insurance instead of paying the tax penalty, due to the youth and salaries of his employees. None of her clients who currently offer insurance have decided to stop doing so."

For suggestions to our readers who are employers, Mrs. Carter stated, "that it is important to keep an open mind and not pre-commit to a compliance path before consulting with your advisor, who can help a business play out various compliance scenarios from both a financial and employee communication perspective." What she was surprised about is that many of her clients are learning that they already have the Human Resource Administration structure needed to continue offering benefits to staff or they simply need to make a few changes to be prepared for the ACA Employer requirements in 2015. She walks her clients through all their compliance options, helping them weigh the value of each element of the "play or pay" decision. She also updates plan documents and Summary Plan Descriptions to reflect changes to their Health Insurance plan.

Waiting Periods

The waiting periods with ACA will change in 2015. Employers will need to adapt their waiting period to the federal maximum time of 90 days. What this means is that companies that have health insurance waiting periods of more than 90 days will need to change their waiting period to 90-, 60- or 30-day waiting periods. Some states can require a different waiting period. California is considering to reduce the waiting period for small and large groups to 60 days.

Auto Enrollment

One part of the ACA that is beneficial for some businesses is that employers who have more than 200 FTE employees can elect to auto enroll staff as soon as they meet the company waiting period.

Employees who choose not to auto enroll into a group health insurance plan can choose to opt out of the option.

ACA Large Group Penalties:

If an employer with more than 50 FTE does not offer group health insurance to its full-time employees, that employer will pay a $2,000 tax penalty per employee not enrolled.

If an employer with more than 50 FTE does not offer group health insurance to its full-time staff and that employee purchases an individual health insurance plan with a federal subsidy, the employer will pay an additional $3,000 tax penalty.

In addition to being ACA compliant, businesses must be compliant with the Employee Benefits Security Administration (EBSA). The EBSA is a division of the Department of Labor and assists employers and employee benefit plan officials in understanding and complying with the requirements of ERISA as it applies to the administration of employee pension and welfare benefit plans. Find out if your company's health insurance plan is Compliant by reviewing the website link to "Self-Compliance Tool for Part 7 of ERISA Affordable Care Act Provisions" in our book Appendix.[17]

Health Insurance Exchanges

The most common question that I receive from people about Health Insurance Exchanges are, "What are the health insurance exchanges?" A Health Insurance Exchange is a website where individuals and businesses can purchase health insurance online. An Exchange can be public, usually managed by a state agency, or it can be private, usually managed by a business organization. A Health Insurance Exchange is also a place where individuals can qualify for federal subsidies to reduce their monthly premiums.

To help readers understand the intention of a public health insurance exchange, I contacted Michael Lujan of Covered California to discuss the ACA prior to his departure from Covered California in August 2013. Mr. Lujan joined Covered California, the California Health Insurance Exchange, as the director of the Small Group Health Option Program (SHOP) back in June 2012. He was also Covered California's Director of Sales and Marketing. He had this to say: "We are all frustrated by the health care cost." Covered California wants to help make health insurance more affordable and accessible to more people, stating that, "One of the features of the ACA is all health plans will have to provide minimum Essential Health Benefits. Each insurance carrier will have the same criteria structure. All health plans will have to determine these four factors: 1) age 2) location (where you live), 3) if you are single or have a family and 4) if you are a smoker."

He continued, "Some ways that employers can adapt and prepare for regulations in regard to the enrollment periods is to work with a licensed professional who will guide the business owners through the options inside and outside the exchange. An important decision that employers must make is whether they want to work with someone who is on top of, up to date and qualified to help navigate them through their options. Not all agents are equally skilled and trained on the topic of the ACA Health Reform."

He went on to say, "Small businesses are currently not and will continue to not be required to offer health insurance to their staff. Small business should be asking why do we offer it now. The reason why most small businesses offer insurance is because they want to attract and maintain quality workers and for morale and the overall compensation and benefit. I believe these things will stay true through 2015."

ACA Health Reform Time Line

Some people are not clear on what and how the ACA has changed our health care, so I will discuss some of the key parts of the monumental law in a timeline.

2010

Dependent coverage up to their 26th birthday for any employee's child will allow more parents to keep their children covered. Children who are 26 years or younger will be permitted to remain on their parent's individual and group health insurance coverage. Prior to this law, dependents were able to stay on the group plan until they met the state's limitation for dependent coverage. For example, in California, parents could keep their dependents children on health insurance plans until they were 19 years old. If that child was in college, then they could stay on the plan until the age of 23 years old. In New Jersey, dependent children could stay on a parent's health insurance plan until the age of 30. Each state would manage the dependent age, and now the federal government requires that an employer in any state has to offer dependent coverage to children aged 26 who may or may not be enrolled in college.[18]

In addition, Medicare prescription drug "donut hole" beneficiary rebates will be given to seniors on Medicare who have a supplemental Part D plan. This part of the bill will pay policy owners a portion of the money they paid to pay for the Medicare care Part D donut hole. A Medicare supplemental plan is a private insurance plan that supplements Medicare coverage that Medicare, a federal health insurance plan, does not cover. A Medicare Part D plan is the drug plan that is required to purchase prescription drugs. This gap in coverage is called a "donut hole." Similar to a deductible, the donut must be met before policy holders receive discounts on their prescription drugs. Once the policy holders meet their prescription drug "donut hole," then the insurance coverage pays for the remaining drugs for that calendar year. For many years, there have been numerous complaints from seniors about the high cost that they need to pay for drugs before the insurance coverage kicks in. As a result, Health and Human Services, a federal agency, has proposed to create a rebate for these participants. The ACA provided a one-time $250 rebate in 2010 to assist Medicare Part D recipients who have reached their Medicare drug plan's coverage gap. This payment was not taxable.

2010 continued

- Small business tax credits are available to qualified employers who have fewer than 25 full-time employees or a combination of full-time and part-time (for example, two part-time employees equal one full time employee for purposes of the credit); the average annual wages of employees must be less than $50,000; and the employer must pay at least half of the insurance premiums. The employer must also pay premiums under a "qualifying arrangement." Only premiums paid by the employer under a qualified arrangement are counted. If the employer provides more than one type of coverage or if the employer's health insurance provider does not charge the same premium for all enrolled employees, the employer may qualify even if it paid less than 50 percent of the premium cost for some employees.[19]

- Temporary high-risk pool is created. The health reform law created a temporary national high-risk pool called the Pre-Existing Condition Insurance Plan (PCIP). This plan provides health coverage to people with pre-existing medical conditions who have been uninsured for six months and have been declined coverage from an insurance carrier because of their pre-existing condition prior to applying for health insurance coverage. The PCIP is a temporary measure designed to bridge the gap until the implementation of other coverage provisions in the law that will take effect in January 2014.

2011

-Prohibition and pre-existing condition exclusion went into effect. Group health plans cannot exclude those who enroll in a plan. Enrollees can include employee spouses or other direct blood relations from the current or previous marriage, which include sons and daughters. The prohibition and pre-existing condition exclusion benefits individuals who are under 19 years old applying for an individual plan. A good example of this change is a kid under the age of 19 years old with cancer cannot be excluded from getting health insurance coverage based on the illness.

-No lifetime or annual limits on health plans went into effect. This part of the law restricts health insurance companies from imposing lifetime benefit maximums on their policyholder's health insurance benefits. Before this portion of the law, insurance carriers would have $5 or 6 million dollar lifetime benefit maximums for subscribers. For example, if a policyholder's medical bills exceeded $5 or 6 million dollars, then the insurance company would no longer pay for that policyholder's medical bills. Since that policyholder was ill other insurance carriers would not accept health insurance applicants because that subscriber was considered to have a pre-existing condition. As a result the policyholder would have to pay for the additional cost for medical bills after they reached their insurance carrier's lifetime benefit maximum.

2012

-New tax ($2 per enrollee) on private health insurance policies that is paid by the insurance carriers will go towards paying for establishing public health insurance exchanges

2014

-All insurance carriers will be required to accept applicants with pre-existing conditions.

- Small business tax credit allows eligible companies to collect tax credits of 35 percent of health insurance expenses. After 2014, the tax credit jumps to 50 percent. The 50 percent credit can be for any two consecutive years. Opposed to tax deductions, the credit allows businesses to get a credit toward taxes already owed.

-The U.S. Department of Health and Human Services will begin to review, test, and approve new state health insurance exchanges in late 2013. The health insurance exchanges are where individuals and businesses will shop for state-qualified and -approved health insurance plans online. Some state exchanges, such as Utah, are already in use. States like California and Utah will be ready for individuals and small group use in October 2013. The Health and Human Services agency requires that all states establishing a health insurance exchange must have a fully functional health insurance exchange available for the public in the fall of 2013. The health exchanges will also be a place where low-income employees can receive government subsidies to help pay for some of their health insurance premium cost.

-The third mandate was postponed from the health insurance reform for now. At the requests of business owners, President Obama repealed the 1099 reporting requirement in 2012. In this portion of the bill, businesses would have been required to report payments in excess of $600 for service or merchandise they received to the Internal Revenue Service on a form 1099. Lots of paper, waste, and frustration would have been created by this part of the law.

2014 Insurance Mandates & Penalties

-Individuals without health insurance with "Essential Health Benefits" coverage are subject to a fine of $95 or one percent of that taxpayers' annual income, whichever is greater. The fines will increase from 2014 to 2015. In 2014, it will be 2% and in 2015, it will be 5% of annual income.

-States deadline to have health insurance exchanges established is mandated by the federal government. If a particular state does not have a state exchange established by 2014, it will only be able to offer health insurance outside of the exchange since the federal exchanges will be unavailable until 2015 because the federal government is not ready to establish one by its original deadline.

-All non-Grandfathered and health insurance exchange plans will be required to meet the health reform mandated level of coverage.

2014 continued

-A tax credit will be available to lower income applicants who fall between 133-400% below the federal poverty level. An example of meeting the level would be a family of three making less than $18,310 and a family of five making less than $25,790 in 2013-2014 income tax years. I don't know many of these people, but I am sure there are many individuals and families who will qualify for these benefits once the health exchanges are up and running in 2014. But if they are making so little, will they be able to afford to pay for benefits even if they get the tax credit? We will just have to wait and see what the future holds.

2015

-Employers with more than 50 *Full-Time Equivalent* (FTE) employees who fail to offer group health insurance that cost no more than 9.5 percent of an employee's annual W-2 income coverage would pay a $3,000 penalty for each employee that receives a subsidy through the health insurance exchange.

Employers with more than 50 *Full Time Equivalent* (FTE) who do not offer group health insurance will pay a tax penalty of $2,000 for every (FTE)

2018

-High-cost employer sponsored health coverage excise tax- also known as the Cadillac excise tax, will be charged to employers if they pay more than $10,200 for each employee and $27,500 for each employee and their family health insurance premiums per calendar year. This law encourages the insurance carriers to keep premiums down for employers and their employees by forcing insurance carriers to keep plan designs simple and effective to serving the consumer needs. At a glance of this interesting design, it looks like the U.S. government pulled it from another country's health insurance system and is making an attempt to transplant here without making an attempt to review the difference between our size and our culture in the United States compared to the other country.

Keep in mind that the regulations that you see in this book today may not be true tomorrow because of edits in the law. If you haven't noticed, many provisions are very confusing and can be very harmful on businesses who may need to pay more in health insurance premiums, not by choice, but because the government regulations, health care costs, and inflation. For example, I predict that health insurance premiums will cost more than the Cadillac tax amounts of $10,200 per individual coverage and $25,500 per family coverage. If there are complaints from consumers about this part of ACA, that part of the law is likely to disappear.

Employer Reporting Tool

If you are an employer or an HR manager who needs assistance with understanding which employees you will need to report their insurance plans to the IRS. I have listed an IRS Employer Reporting Tool called "Reporting and Disclosure Guide for Employee Benefit Plans" website link in this book Appendix.

In 2015, ACA requires employers to report the cost of coverage under an employer-sponsored group health plan. I recommend that readers go to the Internal Revenue Services "Form W-2 Reporting of Employer-Sponsored Health Coverage." I have provided a website link to it in this book Appendix.[20]

ACA Benefits

I will briefly discuss the ACA Health Reform benefits and the challenges that I highlighted earlier. One of the benefits of this law is to ensure that those who are already covered by a health insurance plan are not dropped by their insurance carriers unexpectedly. Prior to this law, insurance carriers would routinely terminate a policy holder's coverage who would have very expensive health procedures, such as cancer treatment or heart surgeries, without notice. This practice is called dropping coverage. This practice was used by many insurance carriers, who would find minor reasons to drop policyholders because they had large medical claims that needed assistance with payment from the insurance carriers but the these insurance carriers did not want to pay them. When the U.S. government began to investigate thousands of reports of this practice, they began to increase fines and stop insurance carriers from selling insurance entirely for a certain amount of time as penalty. ACA makes this practice illegal.

An added benefit to some is the unisex rates. Unisex rates are when an insurance carrier charges the same rate for men and women. Eleven years ago when I transitioned into assisting clients with their health insurance needs, the rates for a male cost more than for a female. Men were known to not visit a doctor until they noticed a chronic or critical health issue. This practice would drive up the cost of insurance because there was not a way to prevent these conditions with any level of intensity because most men did not see a doctor on a regular basis. This meant they could not be notified of a condition at its early stages to cure or prevent it entirely. Most women would visit a doctor at least once or twice a year and did get advice on a condition. Thus, they had the time to be proactive on the proper route of treatment before a condition got to a critical state. Then in the early 2000s, insurance carrier figured out that even through women did have the ability to treat health issues prior to their critical state, women used the insurance more than men, which also drove up the cost of insurance. Shortly after this development, the insurance rates for women were more expensive for women because of high utilization and maternity coverage. After ACA, the unisex rates are the same for each gender and include maturity coverage.

Another new benefit of the ACA law is for individuals who are 19 years or younger. Adults and children with pre-existing conditions, for example, asthma, cancer, or mental illness can purchase health insurance plans on a guaranteed issuance basis. An insurance carrier cannot decline coverage because of a person's previous or current illness. Contact your insurance carrier in your state to find out if there are enrollment period and restrictions that apply.

ACA Benefits cont

ACA was created to make an attempt to encourage businesses to purchase group health insurance plans by providing tax credits for business owners. Any business owners who pay their employees less than $50,000 in annual W-2 income are eligible for this tax credit through their accountant. I have some clients who were on the fence about providing group health insurance to their workers as opposed to a cash contribution to the workers to buy their own individual plans. Most of those clients were won over when I told them about the tax credit and the additional health insurance benefits with a group plan that they were missing.

Let's look at the changes in the benefit design of health insurance plans. The ACA health reform law created the Standard of Benefits, also known as Essential Health Benefits. In 2014, this new benefit design will be mandatory through Grandfathered and non-Grandfathered insured plans in the individual and small group markets in and out of the exchange. Essential Health Benefits will help policy holders with controlling their out-of-pocket health insurance cost and provide necessary health care. Essential Health Benefits must include items and services within at least the following 10 categories: ambulatory patient services; emergency services; hospitalization; maternity and newborn care; mental health and substance use disorder services, including behavioral health treatment; prescription drugs; rehabilitative and habilitative services and devices; laboratory services; preventive and wellness services and chronic disease management; and pediatric services, including oral and vision care." [21] Insurance policies will be required by the ACA law to include these benefits in plans in order to be certified and offered in the Health Insurance Marketplace, and all Medicaid state plans must cover these services by 2014.

Another benefit is keeping dependents on an insurance plan with parent until the age of 26 years old. Prior to this change in the law, children could stay on their parent's insurance until 19 in some states and 21 years old in others. This law mandates the minimum amount of time an adult child can enroll or remain on their parent's insurance.

The ACA has changed the way that physicians interact and manage their patients. One of the ways that the health care system is paying the physicians for assisting patients with improving care and making healthier life choices. Health and Human Services has developed the ACA to hold physicians and hospitals accountable for giving patients access to health care treatment that will cut cost and provide positive results in patient health. One of the ways that they are doing this is by offering employers tax credits for creating an in-house wellness program. These programs must have a benchmark system and tracking to show that participants make health progress from the beginning to the end. Another way that Health and Human Services is changing the way physicians practice Western medicine is by coordinating care to ensure that patients, especially the chronically ill ones, get the right care at the right time while avoiding unnecessary duplication of services and reducing or even preventing medical errors. When a hospital or physician succeeds in meeting both the delivery of high-quality care and reducing the health care cost, they achieve Health and Human Services benchmarks of being successful. Sounds great, but how is this new health care structure working out?

I had the pleasure of interviewing Tim Rice, the President and CEO of the Lakewood Health Care System of Staples, Minnesota, to find out. He has been with Lakewood Health Care Systems since 1980. Since ACA, he mentioned that he is busy trying to structure and focus on the value for patients. In some ways, the hospital has been meeting some regulations and working to engage staff in the process. In the process, he has reduced hospitalization and ER activity up to 50%. The key concept is how they engaged in their health. In the future, the hospital plans to reduce overall cost by 30%.

"I predict that the overall cost of health care will not go down because hospitals are going to be providing more care." Tim Rice stated, "Even though health care providers will be cut by 20 or 30%, there are so many unknowns of how this process is going to go through. For Hospital employees there is a lot of uncertainty."

A great resource for Hospital administrators who want to motivate and prepare staff on the ACA health reform, I have included the "In Search of Joy in Practice: A Site-visit Analysis of Twenty-three Highly Functional Primary Care Practices" website link in our book Appendix. [22]

ACA Challenges

After my interview with Tim Rice and understanding how the health care system will change, it is evident that doctors will be paid for improving a person's care, which will be a challenge for doctors and their patients. One of the reasons is that patients are used to telling the doctor what they want, and most doctors simply give it to them. Doctors will no longer be able to follow the previous health care model and will not be able to discuss the reasons because, in most cases, it is inappropriate to discuss with patients, especially because patients will not need to know that these changes will affect the way they receive doctor care.

Another challenge that I see being evident is how physicians care for the millions of new patients with fewer staff and less resources. Americans should let Health and Human Services know that the health care model that may have modeled after the National Health Service located in the United Kingdom (U.K.) with a population of 61 million may not be the best fit for the United States (U.S.) with 305 million as of 2009. The expectations of health care in the US are different then the UK at a cultural level. Most people in the US expect the best care no matter what. As a result, there are instances when a physician must accept, for example, a 100-year-old patient requesting surgery to remove cancer knowing the procedure is likely to only prolong that patient's life for approximately 3 months and cost insurance companies, insurance policyholders, and Health and Human Services $125,000 or more. Why is this case? For one Medicare and some insurance plans cannot legally deny patient request for care. In contrast, this same patient in the UK would not have an option to receive treatment because of the patient's age and the overall circumstances. The culture in the UK accepts this as a part of their overall health care system. In the US, Americans have a higher expectation of the quality of care regardless of what stage a patient is in life and the cost to maintain their own or a family member's overall health. These factors along with the increasing size of the US's elderly population increase insurance premiums for everyone.

Other challenges facing ACA are the number of doctors retiring from the medical profession as an alternative to not knowing how they will fit into this new health insurance system. I have talked to many doctors and most of them plan to retire before 2014 instead of navigating the new system. The shortage of doctors in the system will cause issues. How do older doctors train new doctors when there is a shortage? How will people receive care when doctors are over-extended and over-worked? What is the incentive for doctors and hospitals to stay in the U.S. health care system as opposed to practicing internationally where there are very fewer regulations telling them how to care for their patients? The answers to those questions will be known after 2014.

The challenge Americans face is that a shortage of doctors will increase patient wait times for services. Most people that I have talked to about the changes to our health care system never thought about how their wait times for doctor visits and surgeries will increase. This will be the result if there are more people coming into the health care system and a shortage of doctors, especially for minor and major surgeries.

The next challenge is that employers may have to pay more to offer employee coverage. Even though the Obama administration announced in July 2013, that the employer mandate for the "play or pay" portion of the health care law will be delayed from 2014 to 2015, it is likely employers will still pay more than they are paying now for health insurance contributions in 2015. This increase will cover the additional cost of the insurance for additional, mandated benefits and taxes. The Obama administration mentioned that the reason for the delay was that employers needed more time to prepare for ACA employer mandates. "Employers with more than 50 *full-time employees* were concerned with the burdensome reporting requirements under the law, a complaint the Administration is particularly sensitive to. Companies that don't meet the law's requirements now have an extra year to alter their policies."[23]

Even though the "play or pay" regulations are delayed for a year, other pieces of the law still exist that have an effect. These include the following:

- Guaranteed issuance for individuals and families

- Essential Health Benefits

- State Health Insurance Exchanges will be active

- Individuals will qualify for tax subsides

These mandates will still be in effect in 2014. All other items are delayed until 2015, so it's best not to get your hopes up that the ACA Health Care Reform employer mandate for companies with more than 50 full-time employees will go away. It's likely that the regulations will change from now to 2015, so keep your eyes open for a second edition of this book. My goal is to make sure readers have the basic tools needed to adapt to new ACA health care reform changes closer to 2015.

The ACA is changing our health care system. In the next portion of this book, I will discuss how the ACA is changing the way that hospitals and physicians will manage patient care in the United States.

Hospitals and Physician Changes

With ACA, there are many regulations that most are not aware, and may have never been aware of, if they didn't read this book. There will be some major changes within our hospital system. Hospitals that can't keep up with the U.S. government regulations and financial requirements are at risk of going out of business.

Since ACA was signed into law in 2010, I have noticed more and more doctors selling their practices to large hospitals like UCLA and Cedar Sinai, or they have simply sold their practices and retired. For those who stay in practice, those who are able to stay up to date with the many regulations that are coming to them as well as have the money to invest in the business regulations will be better off than those who don't. Some of the regulations that doctors will need to have in place in 2014 include a new Electronic Patient Information Systems like Electronic Health Records (EHS) and Electronic Medical Records (EMR). An EMR contains the standard medical and clinical data for a patient gathered in one provider's office. "Electronic health records (EHR) go beyond the data collected in the provider's office and include a more comprehensive patient history that usually includes patient information for many doctors, hospitals, home health centers or hospice care centers."[24] The goal is to put these systems in place to help with coordinating care between all medical professionals handling the care of a patient with the tools that will allow them to provide faster, more effective, and more efficient care.

As I mentioned before, change is difficult for many people. Some enjoy it, and some resist it. In any market, there will be people who will resist and make things difficult for all concerned. Resistance will be evident with many physicians and patients because they are not able to adapt to the overall changes that happen in the U.S. health care system, and as a result, there will be many angry and frustrated people who make the task of implementing the ACA. Be aware of the conflict and continue moving forward to communicate about the ACA to government officials and focus on the law's need for improvement if needed.

Changes in the hospital and physician structure will take time for everyone to get used to, so patience, collaboration, and honesty from Health and Human Services, hospitals, physicians, and patients on what works and what does not is important for the success of our new health care system. If any of these elements are missing, the ACA could be a train wreck waiting to happen.

Why was the ACA created?

The ACA Health Reform was created to fix the current health care system, which has been broken for a long time. Some may deny that change is needed because, for most, it's a very scary thing, especially when most involved can't see results up front and don't understand what is happening at the time, but the change, ACA health reform, is here to stay.

The U.S. government and insurance carriers have mentioned in the media that if there are more people in the health care system, the overall rates for policy owners will stabilize. Please note that they did not say that policyholders would receive reduced rates. For those who believe the ACA health reform will cut health care cost and everything will stay the same, I have some bad news for you new health benefits in health insurance plans, regulations, taxes, and the overall health care system will change. These changes will not be cheap for consumers. The days of cheap health insurance are over. In reality, prices for groceries, cars, human capital, and medical advances increase. Add inflation and demand and costs increase even more. Health care in the United States is no different. Don't get me wrong, I am not saying that I am for nor am I against the ACA health care reform. I am for whatever will have the best results in protecting people in the United States from financial hardship.

Tax Changes

Gregg Wind- Partner - Wind & Stern, Limited Liability Partnership (LLP). Mr. Wind provides tax planning, tax preparation, and estate planning services to small- and medium-sized businesses and their owners and to high net worth entrepreneurs and investors. During our discussion, I asked him the following questions: 1) What new tax changes should business owners and individual and families know about now? 2) Will individuals and families who make a certain amount of income pay more in taxes because of ACA? 3) How much will individuals pay in a tax penalty if they do not purchase health insurance in 2014? 4) What are some benefits and challenges that you believe business owners will have with the new tax structure? 5) Any recommendations on ways business owners, individual and families can prepare for these changes?

In response to my first question Mr. Wind replied "The Affordable Care Act (ACA) is a significant body of work. It contains 47 tax provisions and a myriad of changes in procedure that are likely to redefine the way that individuals and businesses will think about health insurance. Two of the most talked-about aspects of the new law is the mandate that companies with more than 50 full-time employees will be required to provide health insurance to their employees (an employee is defined as one who works more than

120 hours each month) and the requirement that all individuals, except for families that have less than $10,000 of annual income per family member, will be required to maintain health insurance."

In response to my second question, Mr. Wind replied "Generally speaking, tax rates have increased in 2013, as compared to 2012. The top federal tax rate for individuals last year was 35%. This year, the top federal tax rate is 39.6%. Additional taxes that are related to the ACA include a Net Investment Income Tax of 3.8% (this would be in addition to one's regular income tax), which would be assessed on items such as interest and dividend income. The Net Investment Income Tax would apply to folks who file "single" and have income over $200,000 and those who file "married" and have income over $250,000. There is also a new additional Medicare Tax of .9% that applies to both wages and self-employment income and is subject to the same income thresholds for single and married filers. Both the Net Investment Income Tax and the additional Medicare Tax start in 2013."

In response to my third question Mr. Wind replied "While the penalties might not seem onerous to some, in 2014, families that don't have insurance will pay a penalty of $95 per adult and $47.50 per child. So a family of four would pay $285 in penalties. The penalties are capped at 1% of income. If still uninsured in 2015, the penalties jump to $325 per adult and $162.50 per child, so the same uninsured family of four would pay $975 in penalties. And the income cap goes up to 2%. In 2016, higher still, the same family of four would pay $2,085 in penalties with a 2.5% income cap. Apparently, these penalties will not apply to people who file "single" and have less than $10,000 of income and those who file "married" and have less than $20,000 of income."

In response to my fourth question, Mr. Wind mentioned "A major benefit, associated with the ACA, is that everyone will now qualify for health insurance coverage. In the past, those with pre-existing conditions could be denied coverage. Studies have shown that a significant majority of the companies that employ more than 50 people are already paying for health insurance for their employees. The challenge for the companies that are not is how the additional cost of the insurance could impact the salaries that they pay. Salary, health insurance, and other employee benefits could ultimately be viewed as a "compensation package." Employers will also have to make sure that they purchase qualifying insurance (as defined by the ACA) for their employees. It is believed that qualifying insurance must cover at least 60% of an average person's medical costs."

For his last question, he stated "Business owners and individuals alike should take a little time to become familiar with the ACA. A recent Kaiser Foundation poll found that four out of ten surveyed were not even aware that the ACA was part of current law. These business owners and individuals may wish to consider meeting with a qualified health insurance professional to see what their coverage options and related costs are expected to be. Among the various items currently being discussed is whether the current "high deductible" health plans, popular with those that also maintain Health Savings Accounts because annual premiums are typically lower than with a more conventional "co-pay" health insurance policy, would be considered as "qualifying insurance" if, for example, a family had only minimal medical expenses in a given year and perhaps received no reimbursement under the terms of their high deductible policy."

Just to lighten things up here is a summary of ACA employer options:

- Paying for staff health insurance and mandates to be ACA compliant = Apples

• Paying for ACA tax penalties to the IRS = Oranges.

The key is what is best for a particular employer and their staff.

Business "must haves" for
ACA Compliance

- A knowledgeable accountant who shows they understand and can communicate changes in the tax codes because there are many items that businesses will no longer be able to deduct and processes that are required to properly file information to IRS about the ACA on a regular basis.

- A payroll company who is an expert in client software simplicity, excellent client care, and ACA updated notices to keep track of staff income, amounts that should be paid for insurance benefits, and last but not least, notice of the various employee health insurance waiting periods.

- An insurance advisor who is proactive, educated on the health care system and new and existing products, and can educate clients on things employers must know to protect their assets and eliminate the risk of paying penalties to the IRS and Department of Labor. If your insurance advisor is a great friend, but not your advocate, then it is time for a change. If they are not looking out for you and your interest now, then it is likely that will do more of the same later.

- Protect yourself and make needed changes so your company is prepared to have a trouble-free experience with the ACA.

Simplify ACA regulations for employers with more than 50 FTE

There is much confusion on what an employer must do with the ACA reform. I have seen some of my clients just freeze up, and I have guided them through the right steps to make sure they are compliant with the Department of Labor. I also have clients who are ready to take the regulations apart and implement everything that is needed to make sure they are compliant. Here is a list of things to do to make it easier to focus on what is important in the ACA to make sure an employer is compliant.

Once the employer decides if they will "play or pay" with the ACA Health Care Reform then the next step is to make sure they are compliant.

The first step is to simplify the requirements by hiring a payroll company that will help track the enrollment periods and employee contribution amounts for you at no additional cost. A good payroll company can provide you up–to-date changes in the laws. Most of the time, the government will change laws, and in most cases, the way an employer finds out about the changes is by a professional in that specific area. Use a payroll company that will keep you posted on these changes so that you are not left holding a bill you were not expecting.

-Hire a Third Party Administration (TPA) that specializes in group health insurance and other related employee benefits perks. For example, a group health insurance TPA can ensure that your employee contributions to the insurance have completed the proper paperwork with state agencies to deduct employee benefits on a pre-tax basis. This ability allows for happier employees who are paying less in taxes per paycheck because the employer is deducting employee contributions on a pre-tax basis. The employer is also a happy camper; since the employee is paying less in taxable income, the overall FICA and worker's compensation cost is less than without this feature. Another item that a TPA can implement is Health Benefits Security Project (HBSP) compliance. Managed by the Department of Labor and established in 2012, the Health Benefits Security Project (HBSP) is Employee Benefits Security Administration (EBSA). *EBSA* provides participant and compliance assistance regarding pension, health and other employee benefit plans HBSP provides comprehensive national health enforcement project, combining EBSA's established health plan enforcement initiatives with the new protections afforded by the Patient Protection and Affordable Care Act of 2010 (ACA). The HBSP involves a broad range of health care investigations, including examinations for compliance with ERISA and ACA to ensure that promised benefits are actually provided.[25] There are EBSA and ERISA compliance packages that a business can purchase that have all required items to ensure the group is compliant for a nominal annual fee. When a company hires a TPA to manage the company's EBSA compliance requirement plan, they will save significant amounts of money. The Department of Labor can charge up to $2000 each day a company is not EBSA compliant. A company is better safe to have a TPA take that liability than to be sorry that it paid money for ACA compliance penalties.

To ensure that large groups are complaint with ACA they will have the following things to do when enrolling eligible staff into their group health insurance plans:

-Pick the method of enrollment. A company will have choices on where they want to enroll their staff in health insurance plans in 2015. One choice is a private health insurance exchange. Aon Hewitt, a worldwide insurance firm, and Mercer, an executive and employee benefits consulting firm that also handles insurance services, will have private health insurance exchanges available to their large group clients. The second option is to contact an insurance carrier or broker to enroll in a group plan outside of a health insurance exchange. The third option was recently eliminated in the summer of 2013. Health and Human Services announced that the federal health insurance exchange would delay enrollment until sometime in 2017. Since the U.S. presidential and senate elections are in 2016, there is a risk of the new president and members having a different agenda. It's difficult to predict that the Federal Exchange will be something that is actually created and utilized.

Once employers decide the route they want to take to establish health insurance benefits, the next step would be to manage the benefits plan with the following items to ensure they will avoid penalties:

- For companies who have 200 and more employees, they can select automatic enrollment for new employees who meet the required waiting period. The group must give the employee at least 30 days to opt out of this option.

- A business must provide the Department Labor with business information, such as the summary of benefits and coverage, waiting periods, and health insurance plans offered to employees of that company. They may also ask for the premium amounts for each employee's insurance and each employee's insurance portion.

Since there are many things to be ready to implement correctly, it is essential that an employer has a good insurance professional, human resource staff, and payroll and tax person communicating to make sure they can assist a business owner with meeting these requirements.

If you are not sure if your current providers have the knowhow to provide you with excellent service, keep you informed, and be your advocate, feel free to make a change by switching that provider before 2015. The last thing business owners want is a nice penalty because they stuck with a professional who was a friend opposed to someone who was a specialist in their field. Change is difficult sometimes, but it is needed to move on to greater things.

Purpose

As a risk manager and client advocate, I love to educate, advise, and implement whatever is the best fit for most concerned. That is why I have chosen to help others navigate through America's complex health care system. I choose to be a part of this goal because, when I was 17 years old, my father died of pancreatic cancer. Luckily, my mom and dad had health and life insurance to pay some of the bills. The one thing that was missing was an insurance advisor who could have helped us put a health insurance plan into place that made it so that we could afford the out-of-pocket cost of our share of health insurance bills from my father's cancer treatments.

The other thing that person could have helped us with was encouraging my parents to buy enough life insurance to help pay our share of health insurance costs and replace the income that my mom depended on when my father was alive to pay the overall bills and unexpected expenses and taxes. As a result of not having an advisor to help us with these needs, my mother had to file for bankruptcy. We were forced to leave our home because we could no longer pay for it. As a result of that experience, my life's purpose is to help others in the way that I wished that I was helped when my father died. I met many people who work day-to-day just to get a pay check, who are not interested in finding their passion and purpose. I just so happen to be lucky to have found mine.

This book represents an opportunity for Americans who serve others to assist them with understanding changes in the country's health care system driven by the ACA. For example, health care professionals working as client advocates and experts in their field will lead with their morals, values and integrity. Using this book they will be successful in adapting and implementing ACA's required reforms. In the end, I hope that in 2024, Americans can look back at the old system and say, "Thank goodness we made the switch to a new and improved health care reform system. The U.S. is much better off now with the new health care system than ever before."

The End

The End

Endnotes

1. Jaspen, B. (2012) HMOs Decline, Consumer Plans Rise As Health Insurance Option. Forbes Magazine, 149. Retrieved from www.forbes.com/sites/brucejapsen/2012/09/17/hmo-declines-consumer-plans-rise-as-health-insurance-option/2/

2. Children Health Insurance Plan (2013) Retrieved from http://www.medicaid.gov/medicaid-chip-program-information/by-topics/childrens-health-insurance-program-chip/childrens-health-insurance-program-chip.

3. What's the Part D late enrollment penalty (2013) retrieved from www.medicare.gov/part-d/costs/penalty/part-d-late-enrollment-penalty.html

4. Closing the Coverage Gap ,Medicare Prescription Drugs Are Becoming More Affordable http://www.medicare.gov/Publications/Pubs/pdf/11493.pdf

5. Keehan, SP et al. 2012. National Health Expenditure Projections: Modest Annual Growth Until Coverage Expands and Economic Growth Accelerates. Health Affairs 31(7). Retrieved from http://content.healthaffairs.org/content/31/7/1600.abstract

6. Agency for Healthcare Research and Quality. Prescription Medicines-Mean and Median Expenses per Person With Expense and Distribution of Expenses by Source of Payment: United States, 2010. Online

7. 2010. Prescription Drug Trends. And IMS Health 2011 Data, 2012. Kaiser Family Foundation.

8. Retrieved by http://www.kaiseredu.org/Issue-Modules/Prescription-Drug-Costs/Background-Brief.aspx#footnote3

9. About us retrieved from http://www.mdvip.com/what-is-mdvip/who-we-are

10. Prescription Drugs: 7 Out Of 10 Americans Take At Least One, Study Finds retrieved from http://www.huffingtonpost.com/2013/06/19/prescription-drugs-prevalence-americans_n_3466801.html

11. Future Growth, Department of Health and Human Services retrieved from http://www.aoa.gov/Aging_Statistics/Profile/2011/docs/2011profile.pdf

12. Future Growth, Department of Health and Human Services retrieved from http://www.aoa.gov/Aging_Statistics/Profile/2011/docs/2011profile.pdf

13. Administration of Aging retrieved from http://www.aoa.gov/Aging_Statistics

14. A profile of Older Americans 2011 retrieved from http://www.aoa.gov/Aging_Statistics/Profile/2011/docs/2011profile.pdf#page=5&zoom=auto,0,740

15. The Accountable Care Fiasco.(2011) The Wall Street Journal. Retrieved from http://online.wsj.com/article/SB1000142405270 23045208045763434107297269144.html

16. Health Care Information for Employers, Massachusetts Department of Revenue (2013) retrieved from http://www.mass.gov/dor/businesses/current-tax-info/health-care-information.html

17. Band, R (2013) 'Walmart Loophole' Allows Big Employers to Undermine Affordable Care Act. AFL –CIO retrieved from http://www.aflcio.org/Blog/Corporate-Greed/Report-Walmart-Loophole-Allows-Big-Employers-to-Undermine-Affordable-Care-Act

18. Self-Compliance Tool for Part 7 of ERISA: Affordable Care Act Provisions, United States Department of Labor retrieved from h ttp://www.dol.gov/ebsa/pdf/part7-2.pdf

19. McQueen, M (2006) More states mandating health coverage for adult children. The Wall Street Journal..Retrieved from http://www.post-gazette.com/stories/news/health/more-states-mandating-health-coverage-for-adult-children-429572/

20. Small Business Health Care Tax Credit Questions and Answers: Who Gets the Tax Credit? Department of Internal Revenue (2013) Retrieved from Small Business Health Care Tax Credit Questions and Answers: Who Gets the Tax Credit

21. W-2 Reporting. Department of Internal Revenue. (2013) retrieved from http://www.irs.gov/uac/Form-W-2-Reporting-of-Employer-Sponsored-Health-Coverage

22. Essential Health Benefits, Health Care.gov retrieved from https://www.healthcare.gov/glossary/essential-health-benefits

23. Sinsky,Willard-Grace, Schutzbank, Sinsky, Margolius,and Bodenheimer (2013) In Search of Joy in Practice: A Report of 23 High-Functioning Primary Care Practices Ann Fam Med May/June 2013 11:272-278; doi:10.1370/afm.1531 retrieved from http://annfammed.org/content/11/3/272.full

24. Miller, Z (2013) Obama Administration Delays Health Care Law Employer Penalty Until 2015. Time.com Retrieved from http://swampland.time.com/2013/07/02/obama-administration-delays-health care-law-employer-penalty-until-2015/#ixzz2Y7qgWSV3

25. What Is an Electronic Medical Record (EMR)?,Healthit.gov retrieved from http://www.healthit.gov/providers-professionals/electronic-medical-records-emr

26. Health Benefits Security Project, Department of Labor Administration retrieved from http://www.dol.gov/ebsa/erisa_enforcement.html